BREAKFAST RECIPES

Easy, Healthy and Tasty Recipes for Your Everyday Cooking

G.S. Williams

All rights reserved.

Disclaimer

The information contained i is meant to serve as a comprehensive collection of strategies that the author of this eBook has done research about. Summaries, strategies, tips and tricks are only recommendation by the author, and reading this eBook will not guarantee that one's results will exactly mirror the author's results. The author of the eBook has made all reasonable effort to provide current and accurate information for the readers of the eBook. The author and it's associates will not be held liable for any unintentional error or omissions that may be found. The material in the eBook may include information by third parties. Third party materials comprise of opinions expressed by their owners. As such, the author of the eBook does not assume responsibility or liability for any third party material or opinions. Whether because of the progression of the internet, or the unforeseen changes in company policy and editorial submission guidelines, what is stated as fact at the time of this writing may become outdated or inapplicable later.

The eBook is copyright © 2020 with all rights reserved. It is illegal to redistribute, copy, or create derivative work from this eBook whole or in part. No parts of this report may be reproduced or retransmitted in any reproduced or retransmitted in any forms whatsoever without the writing expressed and signed permission from the author.

TABLE OF CONTENT

INTRODUCTION

BREAKFAST

Food eaten in the morning is our first source of energy after a long period of fasting. While we sleep, our body continues to need energy, which is obtained from our body's reserves as external sources such as food are available. Hence, it is very common to hear the phrase: "breakfast is the most important meal of the day" and indeed it is for everyone, whether or not they suffer from diabetes, as it provides nutrients and energy to keep the body active throughout the day.

Intellectual and physical performance is higher in children and adolescents who eat breakfast properly. A good breakfast provides 20% to 25% of the daily caloric requirement, which helps to achieve an intake of adequate nutrients such as vitamins, minerals, proteins, carbohydrates and fats.

In addition, both in adults and in children and adolescents, skipping breakfast contributes to a greater probability of suffering from obesity and diabetes.

People who do not eat breakfast are more likely to suffer from obesity since after submitting to prolonged fasts, our body responds by accumulating part of the energy received from the first foods as a reserve in the form of fat.

In addition, the International Diabetes Federation recognizes breakfast as a fundamental part in the prevention and maintenance of people with diabetes, for example, it has been seen that people living with type 2 diabetes who skip breakfast can present high peaks of the blood glucose levels after lunch and dinner.

What breakfasts are not healthy?

The big problem with breakfast is that most people tend to make it with ingredients that are unhealthy. For this reason, many fail to obtain the benefits mentioned. Here are the most common breakfast mistakes today:

Excess of refined carbohydrates: White bread, pastries, pastries, industrial cereals. All of these cause sugar spikes and make us hungry again a short time later. Furthermore, as a study published in The American Journal of Clinical Nutrition points out, they can contribute to obesity and diabetes in the long term.

Excess sugars, especially white sugar: the negative effects that added sugar causes in the body are a matter of controversy. However, research published in Critical Reviews in Clinical Laboratory Sciences suggests that it is linked to an increased risk of obesity and metabolic problems. Therefore, sugary breakfast items are not a good option.

Excess dairy: as long as you do not have an intolerance, dairy can be consumed in moderation. In fact, a study published in Food and Nutrition Review found that they help meet nutrient recommendations and may protect against chronic disease. The mistake that can be made when incorporating them in breakfast is eating them in excessive amounts.

Ultra-processed products: sausages, fried foods, canned goods, pastries and in general any type of ultra-processed product is a bad option for breakfast and the diet in general. They not only contain large amounts of sugars and trans fats, but also chemicals that can affect health.

How to achieve a balanced breakfast?

For a meal to be balanced, it must contain the necessary amounts, no more and no less, of carbohydrates, protein, fat, fiber, and vitamins and minerals. In this way, the body will digest and assimilate it properly, and we will feel that we are with energy and good humor throughout the day.

In addition, we must try that these nutrients are of the highest possible quality. This is feasible if natural and fresh foods are always chosen over those that are processed.

Top 10: Good reasons for a healthy breakfast

Breakfast can be so nice - at an opulently laid table, with freshly squeezed orange juice and oven-warm bakery rolls. Even a tiny espresso with a quick snack is not to be sniffed at. In general, the following applies: Those who have breakfast live healthier. Those who also have a healthy breakfast have a clear advantage - the ten most important reasons for this.

Reason # 1 - the perfect foundation of nutrition

If you start the day with a healthy breakfast, you create a solid basis for all activities. He is immune to food cravings and can work at full capacity for hours. The basis for this positive effect is our blood sugar level, which gradually rises after the "right" breakfast and then only slowly falls again. The "right" stands for protein-rich food with complex carbohydrates. Both are contained in a wholesome muesli with a little yogurt, for example.

Reason # 2 - lose weight in the morning

You can turn it around as you want: We have to use more energy than we consume through food, otherwise there will be nothing with losing weight. However, many factors play a role in energy consumption itself, including the glycemic index. Put simply, it means: If food releases its energy slowly, our internal combustion engine stays going longer.

We feel full and fit, even without further sweets. This criterion is fulfilled, for example, by fruit, which should not be missing on any breakfast table.

Reason # 3 - lose weight and get going

As the "Focus" reported some time ago, Italian universities have shown in tests that breakfast also has a positive effect compared to food abstinence. Those who don't have breakfast at all are more likely to struggle with figure problems than people who traditionally reach for rolls, jam and coffee. Here, too, the reason is that our metabolism does not get going without the energy boost in the morning, which we often feel in the lack of drive. However, the theory of feasting in the morning "like a king" was not confirmed. A light meal to start the day is most effective.

Reason # 4 - fitness and mental strength

Beyond calories, carbohydrates and vitamins, a healthy breakfast has another, often underestimated effect: it gives us the time to collect ourselves so that we can concentrate and confidently go about our day's work. Anyone who rushes at breakfast is wasting the chance to avoid mistakes through hectic actionist. The time we spend on breakfast is well invested.

Reason # 5 - the way of life

A healthy breakfast has style. Style is neither tested in exams nor graded at university, but it does decide about our job and career - often at least, mostly we just don't know anything about it. By the way, our individual lifestyle also determines our happiness. A healthy breakfast is not only stylish, it also makes you happy.

Reason # 6 - Vitamins for Fitness

Eat vitamins, it was said from childhood. Rightly so, because our fitness and well-being depend on it. Vitamins are part of the start of the day, and fruit isn't the only source of them. Whole grain products contain a lot of vitamin B and muesli is rich in vitamin E. Our body needs both for the metabolism to protect the cells.

Reason # 7 - breakfast is a matter of taste

The Germans are regarded as grumpy breakfasters, even in European comparison. According to a survey by the market research institute Metrix LAB, six percent of Germans do without it completely. Other studies assume far higher numbers. Above all, the enjoyment factor could change this - because a healthy breakfast can definitely taste good. What counts is the individual taste and the knowledge of the possibilities, because almost every favorite breakfast can be made healthy. You just have to know how and take the time to prepare.

Reason 8 - the variety of healthy breakfasts

Whether muesli, smoothie, scrambled eggs, steak or snacks, whether at the kitchen table or from the large buffet, breakfast has many variations. Those who keep reinventing their breakfasts bring variety to the day, especially on weekends. So, you can confidently have a full breakfast as a drink and still do something for your health. The possibilities for scrambled eggs alone are limitless, extra ingredients such as herbs and tomatoes ensure taste and healthy ingredients.

Reason # 9 - socializing

In families in particular, meals are often the only opportunity to come together and exchange a few words. However, this opportunity is only used by 41 percent of parents, according to the result of the Metrix LAB survey, which was started in 2011. Breakfast also becomes a social component, which avoids a number of problems. The short morning conversation is only one component, but one of the foundations.

Reason # 10 - proactively for a healthy breakfast

The preparation of a healthy breakfast - also for weight loss - is therefore easy because there are no ready-made products. Here you almost always mix and sizzle yourself, so you decide what goes into it. In moderation, honey and maple syrup are quite beneficial for fitness and health, as are bacon and smoked fish. Anyone who likes to experiment will learn right away for the next banquet with friends or the Sunday brunch.

An optimal breakfast should include:

Bread and cereals preferably whole grains that provide the body with fiber and carbohydrates that provide energy, vitamins and minerals.

Low-fat dairy products that provide protein, calcium and vitamins.

Fruits that provide water, vitamins, minerals and fiber.

Protein foods that provide protein, fat, vitamins, and minerals.

Remember breakfast is part of our healthy habits, do not forget to do it daily.

THE THREE KEY FOODS FOR A GOOD BREAKFAST

Milk or dairy derivatives, such as yogurt or cheese.

The most important property of this group of foods is calcium, and proteins of high biological value. They also contain significant amounts of vitamins A, D, B12, and other minerals such as phosphorus. But they are poor in iron, copper and vitamin C. Milk, in people with overweight and blood lipid alterations, it is advisable to take it semi-skimmed or skimmed, with less fat and, therefore, fewer calories and cholesterol. Yogurt also provides probiotics.

Cereals and derivatives but with fiber, such as whole wheat bread, oatmeal, etc. This type of food mainly provides complex carbohydrates, some protein and little fat, as well as B vitamins and minerals.

They are an important source of energy for the body. The contribution of B vitamins and fiber stands out, especially if they are whole.

Fresh fruit.

They provide water, fiber, vitamins and minerals. Together with vegetables they provide most of the antioxidant substances. They are usually consumed especially at the end of meals because they are very effective in facilitating the assimilation of many nutrients. But they are a very good option not only for breakfast but also for a snack.

The balanced combination of these three food groups provides the basic elements: carbohydrates, fiber, protein, water and the necessary amount of fat. They can be completed with other foods such as dried fruits (walnuts, almonds, hazelnuts), protein foods such as eggs or cheese and fatty foods such as extra virgin olive oil. It is important to remember that the perfect drink to accompany a good breakfast is water.

Foods that should be eaten sporadically, not regularly

One of the mistakes that are usually made at breakfast is to make the consumption of certain foods habitual when in reality its consumption would have to be from time to time. These are foods such as sugar, honey, jam, chocolate, butter, packaged fruit juices, industrial pastries, cookies, sugary breakfast cereals, and cold cuts and other processed meats.

The abuse of this type of food and sugary soft drinks unbalances the normal supply of carbohydrates. What they actually do is provide a large amount of energy (from sugars) without supplying any essential nutrients.

7 things you should know about breakfast

Francis Bacon said that "Hope is a good breakfast but a bad dinner." But in addition to hope, there are other foods that are especially good for us if they are included in the first meal of the day.

Don't skip it.

According to a study, both children and adults who skip the first meal of the day tend to eat worse and lead a more sedentary life. They also tend to have higher cholesterol and insulin levels (and therefore more likely to suffer from diabetes and heart disease) than those who eat breakfast.

Less overweight.

A study by the National Heart, Lung, and Blood Institute (USA) revealed that young women who eat breakfast cereals have a lower waist-height ratio, which is the best indicator of absence of overweight and low cardiovascular risk. Also, a Scraton University study revealed that wheat or corn cereals contain more antioxidants than any other breakfast.

In a meeting.

According to a One Poll survey, meetings during breakfast are more productive than meetings in the afternoon. 67% of the subjects are more predisposed to be attentive during breakfast.

Exercise first.

A recent study from the University of Birmingham published in Medicine & Science in Sports & Exercise It showed that a higher proportion of fat is burned when we exercise before eating breakfast. However, if we eat breakfast first and move later, engineered carbohydrates (cereals, bread, etc.) disrupt fat metabolism for at least 6 hours.

Less lead.

A study in the Environmental Health Journal revealed that children who eat breakfast daily have lower levels of lead in their blood (15% less) than those who skip this meal.

If you are on a diet.

Adults trying to lose weight are more successful eating a healthy breakfast than avoiding it and having something in the middle of the morning. On the other hand, a study by the Pennington Center for Biomedical Research has revealed that eating eggs for breakfast helps to lose between 60 and 65% more weight in subjects who are subjected to a weight loss diet than any other breakfast.

Without breakfast you smoke more.

According to a study published in the European Journal of Clinical Investigation, the absence of breakfast is associated, in addition to being overweight, with a greater tendency to smoke tobacco, consume marijuana and drink alcohol.

BREAKFAST RECIPES

Avocado Salmon Bread

Ingredients for 4 people

- 1-2 tsp peeled sesame seeds
- 2 thin spring onions (approx. 40 g)
- lime
- ripe avocados (approx. 400 g)
- salt and pepper
- 4 slices (80-100 g each) Whole wheat bread with grains
- 6 slices (approx. 150 g) smoked salmon

preparation

15 minutes

1 Roast the sesame seeds in a pan without fat, remove immediately and let cool. Clean and wash the spring

onions, pat dry and cut into fine rolls. Squeeze the lime.

2   Halve the avocados, remove the stone and remove the flesh from the skin with a spoon. Drizzle the avocado pulp with 2 tablespoons of lime juice, season with a little salt and pepper and mash lightly with a fork.

3   Brush bread slices with avocado pulp and cover each with 1 1/2 slices of salmon. Sprinkle with spring onions and sesame seeds.

Nutritional info

1 portion approx:

360 kcal14 g protein16 g fat35 g of carbohydrates

Quinoa porridge with grapes and banana

Ingredients for 4 people

- 250 g Quinoa
- 750 ml Almond drink
- 3 Bananas
- 350 g seedless blue grapes
- 100 g Almond kernels
- 1 tbsp cinnamon
- 4 tbsp Liquid honey

preparation

25 minutes

1   Rinse the quinoa in a colander with warm water. Bring the almond drink and quinoa to the boil in a saucepan while stirring. Simmer on the lowest setting for about 15 minutes, until most of the liquid has been absorbed.
2   Peel the bananas and cut into small pieces. Wash and halve the grapes. Stir half of the bananas and grapes into the porridge, leave to soak for about 5 minutes.
3   Roughly chop the almonds. Add cinnamon and honey to the porridge, arrange in bowls. Place the rest of the grapes and bananas on top and sprinkle with almonds.

Nutritional info

1 person approx:

590 kcal2470 kJ16 g protein19 g fat88 g of carbohydrates

Banana pancakes with blueberry groats

Ingredients for 4 people

- 250 g Blueberries (fresh or frozen)
- 1 tbsp food starch
- 1/4 l Apple juice
- 3 tbsp Maple syrup
- 2 ripe bananas
- 60 g Coconut flour
- 2 tsp baking powder
- cinnamon
- 4th Eggs (size M)
- 1/8 l milk

- 6 tbsp oil
- 250 g Cream curd

preparation

30 minutes

1   Pick and wash fresh blueberries. Mix the starch with 2 tbsp apple juice until smooth. Bring the rest of the juice and maple syrup to the boil, stir in the starch, simmer for about 2 minutes. Add fresh or frozen berries, continue to simmer for approx. 5 minutes. Let the compote cool a little or cool completely.

2   Peel the bananas, grind them with a fork. Mix the flour, baking powder and 1⁄4 teaspoon cinnamon. Whisk eggs, milk and 4 tablespoons of oil, mix with banana puree and flour mix to form a smooth dough.

3   Heat 2 tablespoons of oil in a large pan. Bake 12 pancakes from the batter until golden brown in about 4 minutes, turning once. Serve the pancakes with quark, blueberry compote and possibly banana slices.

Nutritional info

1 portion approx:

520 kcal19 g protein31 g fat37 g of carbohydrates

Scrambled eggs with spring onions on whole meal bread

Ingredients for 1 person

- 2 handle (s) Parsley and dill
- 1 Spring onion
- 1 tomato
- 1 Egg (size M)
- salt
- 1 slice Whole grain bread
- pepper
- oil

preparation

10 mins

1. Wash the herbs, shake dry, pluck the leaves from the stems and chop. Clean and wash the spring onions and cut into rings except for something to garnish. Wash and clean tomatoes, cut 2 slices and dice remaining tomatoes. Whisk the egg and herbs. Season with salt
2. Brush a coated pan with oil and heat. Briefly fry the spring onion rings and diced tomatoes in a hot pan. Season with salt. Add the egg and bring to a stop while stirring
3. Arrange bread, tomato slices and scrambled eggs on a plate. Garnish with spring onions. Season with pepper

Nutritional info

1 person approx:

190 kcal790 kJ12 g protein7 g fat20 g of carbohydrates

Whole grain bread with goat cream cheese, ham and pear wedges

Ingredients for 4 people

- 1 pear
- 4 slices Whole grain bread (approx. 45 g each)
- 2 tbsp Goat cream cheese
- 4 slices Parma ham (approx. 15 g each)
- freshly ground pepper
- preparation

10 mins

1 Wash the pear, rub dry, quarter, remove core and cut fourth into wedges.
2 Spread cream cheese on bread, place ham on top and garnish pear wedges on top. Sprinkle with pepper.

Nutritional info

1 person approx:

150 kcal630 kJ6 g protein3 g of fat23 g of carbohydrates

Whole grain toast with banana, cottage cheese and almonds

Ingredients for 4 people

- 2 Bananas
- 30 g Almond flakes
- 3 tbsp Liquid honey
- 1 (200 g) Mug of grainy cream cheese
- 8 slices Whole grain toast
- cress

preparation

15 minutes

1. Peel the bananas and cut into pieces. Heat a pan, add the bananas, almonds and 2 tablespoons of honey, let caramelize. Mix the cream cheese and 1 tbsp honey.
2. Toast slices of toast, brush with cream cheese and place banana slices on top.
3. Sprinkle with cress.

Nutritional info

1 person approx:

470 kcal1970 kJ14 g protein8 g of fat48 g of carbohydrates

Mango Number bowl with passion fruit recipe

Ingredients for 2 people

- 1 ripe mango
- 2 Passion fruit
- 2 tbsp Linseed flour (health food store)
- 250 g Coconut yoghurt (vegan; e.g. from Alnatura)
- 3 tbsp Brazil nuts
- 2 tsp linseed
- 1 tbsp Coconut chips
- Passion fruit and edible flowers to decorate

preparation

10 mins

1 Peel the mango, cut the pulp from the stone. Cut about ¼ into slices, dice the rest. Halve the passion fruit, scrape out the pulp.

2 Puree the linseed flour, passion and diced mango pulp, mix with coconut yoghurt. Serve with mango slices, Brazil nuts, flax seeds and coconut chips. If necessary, decorate with passion fruit halves and flower petals.

Nutritional info

1 portion approx:

430 kcal10 g protein29 g fat30 g of carbohydrates

Rice pudding with coconut chips topping

Ingredients for 2 people

- 1 tbsp Almonds (skinless)
- 1 tbsp Cashew nuts
- 1 piece (approx. 2.5 cm each) ginger
- 1 tbsp pitted Medjoold dates
- 60 g white basmati rice
- 300 ml Whole milk

- 1/2 teaspoon, heaped Ghee (clarified sweet cream butter)
- 1 tbsp Raisins
- 5 Cardamom pods (whole or just the seeds)
- 1 large pinch of ground turmeric
- 1/2 tsp Coconut oil (optional)
- 1 tsp Coconut chips (optional)
- 1/2 tsp Jaggery (unrefined whole cane sugar made from sugar cane or palm juice; optional)

preparation

35 minutes (+ 60 minutes waiting time)

1. Chop the almonds or cashews and soak in water for about 1 hour. Ginger peel and finely chop. Chop the dates. Rinse the rice in cold water and drain. Put 100 ml of water and the remaining ingredients in a saucepan.
2. Slowly bring the rice to the boil, stirring occasionally. Then simmer for about 20 minutes, until the rice is soft and a thick, creamy paste.
3. For the garnish, if used, cook all ingredients in a small saucepan for 1–2 minutes over medium heat, stirring constantly, until the coconut chips are lightly browned and crispy.
4. Fill the rice pudding into two bowls and, if used, top with the garnish.

TIP: Take it easy: Since the dish contains milk, you should not enjoy it before or after a salty or sour meal - in Ayurveda this would be an unfavorable combination.

Nutritional info

1 portion approx:

370 kcal9 g protein17 g fat43 g of carbohydrates

Hearty pancake tower

Ingredients for 4 people

- 100 g radish
- 1/2 Cucumber
- 300 g cottage cheese
- Salt pepper
- 2 Eggs (size M)
- 1 tbsp sugar
- 5 tbsp oil
- 250 ml milk
- 175 g Flour
- 1 tsp baking powder
- 6 stalk (s) chives

Preparation

30 minutes

1   Wash the radishes, rub dry, clean and roughly grate. Wash the cucumber, rub dry, clean and roughly grate. Mix the cucumber and radish with the cottage cheese. Season to taste with salt and pepper.
2   Mix the eggs, sugar and a pinch of salt with the whisk of the hand mixer until creamy. Stir in 3 tablespoons of oil and milk. Mix the flour and baking powder and stir in.
3   Heat 2 tablespoons of oil in portions in a coated pan (approx. 20 cm in diameter below). Bake a total of 3 pancakes from the batter one after the other over medium heat for approx. 2 minutes on each side until golden brown. Stack the baked pancakes on a preheated plate and keep them warm.
4   Spread the vegetable-cottage cheese mixture on the pancakes and layer them in a tower. Wash the chives, shake dry and cut into fine rolls. Arrange the turrets on a plate, sprinkle with chives and cut into 4 pieces.

Nutritional info

1 portion approx:

430 kcal21 g protein19 g fat41 g of carbohydrate

Vital veggie bagel

Ingredients for 4 people

- 4th Whole grain bagels
- 2 handfuls tender leaf salads (e.g. baby leaf)
- 1 small cucumber
- 50 g Alfalfa sprouts
- 4 tbsp oil
- 4th Eggs (size M)
- Salt pepper
- 1 pack (150 g each) Herbal cream cheese (e.g. from Miree)

preparation

15 minutes

1. If necessary, bake the bagel (see tip). In the meantime, wash the lettuce and spin dry. Wash the cucumber and cut into pieces approx. 9 cm long. Cut each length into approx. 1/2 cm thick slices. Rinse the sprouts in a colander with cold water and allow to drain.
2. In the meantime, heat the oil in a pan and fry 4 fried eggs over medium heat. After about 3 minutes, turn the eggs over and continue frying for about 1 minute. Season with salt and pepper.
3. Slice the bagels horizontally and brush with cream cheese. Top with the cucumber, lettuce, eggs and sprouts. Place the top half of the bagel on top.

TIP: Brush pre-cooked bagel blanks from the supermarket with egg yolk (whisked with 2 tablespoons of whipped cream), sprinkle with chia seeds, oat flakes, sesame seeds, chopped nuts, etc. Bake in the hot oven according to the package instructions.

Nutritional info

1 portion approx:

480 kcal19 g protein21 g fat53 g of carbohydrate

Whole wheat rolls with cream cheese, radishes and sprouts

Ingredients for 1 person

- 1 whole-grain bread rolls
- 2 tbsp (20 g each) Cream cheese preparation (5% fat)
- 5 radish
- 30 g Radish sprouts
- salt

preparation

5 minutes

1 Halve wholemeal rolls and coat both sides with cream cheese. Clean, wash and slice the radishes. Rinse and drain the radish sprouts.
2 Spread the radish slices and sprouts on the lower half of the bun, season with salt and place the upper half on top

Nutritional info

1 person approx:

190 kcal790 kJ11 g protein3 g of fat28 g of carbohydrates

Whole grain bread with avocado and pomegranate seeds

Ingredients for 4 people

- 1/2 pomegranate
- 1 (200 g each) Mug of grainy cream cheese
- 1 (approx. 300 g) avocado
- slices Whole grain bread (approx. 45 g each)
- Chilli flakes

preparation

15 minutes

1   Halve the pomegranate and knock out the seeds with a spoon. Halve the avocado, remove the stone, remove the pulp from the skin and cut into wedges.
2   Brush the bread slices with cream cheese, place the avocado on top like a roof tile and sprinkle with pomegranate seeds and chilli flakes.

Nutritional info

1 person approx:

270 kcal1130 kJ11 g protein16 g fat22 g of carbohydrates

Fruit salad with pistachio nuts and maple syrup

Ingredients for 4 people

- 1 Apple
- 2 Bananas
- Juice of 1/2 lemon
- 1/4 (approx. 250 g) papaya
- 1/4 (approx. 250 g) pineapple
- Persimmon fruit
- 20 g Pistachio nuts
- 4 tsp Maple syrup

preparation

20 minutes

1. Wash, quarter, core and dice the apple. Peel and slice the bananas. Put the fruit in a bowl and drizzle with lemon juice. Peel the papaya, remove the seeds with a spoon. Eighth pulp and cut into slices. Peel and quarter the pineapple and cut out the woody stalk. Cut the pineapple into pieces. Peel persimmon and cut into small pieces. Crush the pistachio nuts in a mortar
2. Mix the apple, bananas, papaya, pineapple and persimmon in a bowl. Spread over 4 bowls. Pour 1 teaspoon of maple syrup over each and sprinkle with pistachio nuts

Nutritional info

1 person approx:

150 kcal630 kJ2 g protein3 g of fat28 g of carbohydrates

Banana and almond smoothie with cocoa nibs

Ingredients for 4 people

- Bananas
- 8 tbsp Almond butter
- 240 ml Almond drink
- 4 tbsp Agave syrup
- 2 tsp ground cinnamon
- 4 tbsp Cocoa nibs
- 4 stems mint

preparation

10 mins

1   Cut 4 bananas into pieces. Finely puree the bananas, almond butter, almond drink, agave syrup and cinnamon. Stir nibs into the smoothie, except for something to sprinkle.
2   Slice 1 banana diagonally and score on one side. Wash the mint and shake dry. Decorate the edges of the glass with banana slices and mint. Divide the smoothie into the glasses and sprinkle with the remaining cocoa nibs.

Nutritional info

1 glass approx:

370 kcal1550 kJ7 g protein20 g fat42 g of carbohydrates

Beetroot and apple smoothie

Ingredients for 3 people

- 1 small beetroot (approx. 130 g each)
- 1 Apple
- 1 carrot
- 1/4 Cucumber
- 2-3 tbsp Lemon juice
- 5 Ice cubes
- 125 ml Apple juice

preparation

10 mins

1   Clean, peel and cut 1 small beetroot (approx. 130 g) into large pieces (careful, it stains strongly! Wear disposable gloves). Wash, quarter and core 1 apple.

2   Peel, wash and cut 1 carrot. Wash 1/4 of the cucumber and cut into pieces. Puree everything with 2-3 tbsp lemon juice, 5 ice cubes and 125 ml apple juice in a high-performance mixer.

Nutritional info

1 glass approx:

80 kcal1 g protein1 g fat16 g of carbohydrates

Happy smoothie bowl with coconut

Ingredients for 4 people

- 375 g Raspberries (fresh or frozen)
- 3 ripe bananas
- 600 ml Coconut or almond drink
- 6 tbsp Melt flakes
- 1 Organic lime
- 60 g Almonds (with skin)
- 40 g Coconut chips

preparation

20 minutes

1. Sort fresh raspberries, wash if necessary. Let frozen raspberries thaw. Peel the bananas and cut into large pieces. Finely puree coconut drink, bananas, 250 g raspberries, melted flakes and half of the lime zest (depending on the sweetness of the berries, season with agave syrup)
2. Roughly chop the almonds. Pour the raspberry mix into bowls. Sprinkle with 125 g of raspberries, almonds, coconut chips and the rest of the lime.

Nutritional info

1 portion approx:

370 kcal8 g protein18 g fat40 g of carbohydrates

Crunchy munchy muesli out of the oven

Ingredients for 15 people

- 250 g Wholegrain spelled flakes
- 100 g roasted unsalted peanuts
- 50 g Sunflower seeds
- 50 g sesame
- 100 g Almonds (with skin)
- 6 tbsp Liquid honey
- anise
- 100 g dried cranberries
- Parchment paper

preparation

20 minutes

1. Preheat the oven (electric stove: 180 ° C / convection: 160 ° C / gas: see manufacturer). Line a baking sheet with parchment paper. Top with wholemeal spelled flakes, peanuts, sunflower seeds, sesame seeds and almonds and mix. Drizzle honey over the mixture and roast in a hot oven for about 12 minutes until crispy.
2. Take the cereal out of the oven. Scatter 1 teaspoon of aniseed over the top, stir in. Bake for another 3 minutes. Stir in the cranberries, cool briefly and, using the baking paper, pour into a tightly closing container. Tastes great with yogurt and berries!

Nutritional info

1 portion approx:

190 kcal7 g protein9 g fat20 g of carbohydrates

Blueberry yogurt cream

Ingredients for 1 people

- 1 heaped teaspoon of crispy oat flakes
- 1/2 Organic lime
- 100 g blueberries
- 4 tsp Liquid honey
- 300 g Skimmed milk yogurt

preparation

10 mins

1 Roast the oat flakes in a small non-stick pan until golden brown, remove and allow to cool. Wash the lime with hot water, rub dry, finely grate the peel and squeeze out the juice. Sort the blueberries, wash and pat dry. Add honey and mash a little
2 Mix the blueberries, lime juice, zest and yogurt together. Pour the yogurt into a bowl and sprinkle with oatmeal

Nutritional info

1 person approx:

270 kcal1130 kJ15 g protein2 g of fat45 g of carbohydrates

Spelled apple muesli with yogurt

Ingredients for 1 person

- 50 g Spelled flakes
- 1/2 tsp Sesame seeds
- 1/2 Apple
- 1 tsp Sultanas
- 1 tbsp low-fat yoghurt
- 1 tsp honey

preparation

15 minutes

1 Roast the spelled flakes and sesame seeds in a pan without fat, turning for about 5 minutes, remove. Quarter the apple, remove the core and dice the pulp, except for a thin apple slice for decoration.
2 Add the sultanas and apple cubes to the pan. Pour 4 tablespoons of water and allow to soak in the closed pan for about 5 minutes. Let cool down. Arrange the muesli and yoghurt in a bowl, drizzle with honey and decorate with apple slices.

Nutritional info

1 person approx:

270 kcal1130 kJ8 g protein3 g of fat52 g of carbohydrates

Papaya with grainy cream cheese

Ingredients for 1 person

- 100 g papaya
- 200 g grained cream cheese
- 2 handle (s) Lemon balm
- 1 tsp Mineral water
- 1 tsp Lemon juice

preparation

10 mins

1   Remove the seeds from the papaya. Peel the pulp
    and cut into cubes. Mix the papaya and cream
    cheese. Wash lemon balm, pat dry, pluck leaves
    from 1 stalk and roughly chop.
2   Stir the leaves, mineral water and lemon juice into
    the cream cheese, arrange and decorate with the
    rest of the lemon balm.

Nutritional info

1 person approx:

220 kcal920 kJ27 g protein9 g fat6 g of carbohydrates

Warming carrot muesli "Sun Salutation"

Ingredients for 2 people

- 200 g Carrots
- 400 ml milk
- 125 g Nut muesli
- 2-3 dried soft figs
- 1 small apple (e.g. Elstar)
- 2 tbsp chopped pistachios

preparation

20 minutes

1   Peel and roughly grate the carrots. Bring the milk to the boil, stir in the muesli and simmer for 1–2 minutes while stirring. Remove from heat, stir in half of the carrots and let soak for about 5 minutes.

2   In the meantime, chop the figs into small pieces. Wash, quarter and core the apple and slice or cut into thin slices. Fill porridge into bowls. Place the apple, figs, pistachios and the rest of the carrots on top. Serve immediately.

Nutritional info

1 portion approx:

380 kcal13 g protein13 g fat50 g of carbohydrates

Perky yogurt with peach and pistachios

Ingredients for 4 people

- 4th ripe peaches (or nectarines)
- 3 tbsp + 4 teaspoons of liquid honey
- cinnamon
- 2 tbsp Lemon juice
- 4-6 tbsp orange juice
- 3 tbsp Wheat Bran or Spelled Bran
- 500 g Greek yogurt (10% fat)
- 4 tbsp Pistachio nuts

preparation

15 minutes

1 Wash, halve and stone the peaches. Roughly dice half of the peaches. Puree with 2 tablespoons of honey, 1 pinch of cinnamon, lemon and orange juice. Stir in bran.

2 Beat the yogurt until smooth. Distribute the yogurt and peach puree alternately in thin layers in 4 glasses. Cut the remaining peaches into narrow wedges. Roughly chop the pistachios. Spread both on the peach yogurt. Drizzle with 1 teaspoon of honey each.

Nutritional info

1 portion approx:

300 kcal7 g protein16 g fat29 g of carbohydrates

Pancake casserole

Ingredients for 4 people

- zwieback
- 200 g Raspberries
- 1 tsp + 3 tbsp Cane sugar
- 1/2 tsp cinnamon
- 1/2 Organic lemon
- 25 g butter
- Eggs (size M)
- 1 pinch salt
- 200 g Ricotta (semi-fat)
- 200 ml + 3 tbsp low-fat milk (1.5%)
- 200 g Spelled flour (type 630)
- 1/2 packet baking powder
- 4 tsp Sunflower oil

- 125 g lowfat quark
- Lemon balm

preparation

50 minutes

1 Put the rusks in a freezer bag and roughly mash them with a rolling pin. Sort out raspberries, wash and drain if necessary. Mix 1 teaspoon sugar and cinnamon together. Wash the lemon with hot water, dry it and finely grate the peel.

2 Melt 15 g butter, let cool. Mix 2 eggs, 2 tbsp sugar, lemon zest and salt with the whisk of the hand mixer until creamy. Stir in the ricotta, melted butter and 200 ml milk. Mix the flour and baking powder and stir in.

3 Heat the oil in portions in a large non-stick pan. Bake 3 pancakes one after the other over medium heat on each side for about 2 minutes until golden brown. Remove from the pan and layer in an ovenproof dish. Makes a total of 12-14 pancakes.

4 Mix the quark, 1 egg, 3 tablespoons milk and 1 tablespoon sugar. Spread the raspberries on the pancakes and pour the quark over them evenly. Spread the rusk crumbles on top and cover with cinnamon sugar. Spread 10 g butter on top and bake in the preheated oven (electric stove: 200 ° C / convection: 175 ° C) on the middle rack for 10–15 minutes. Sprinkle with lemon balm and serve.

Nutritional info

1 portion approx:

500 kcal2100 kJ24 g protein18 g fat57 g of carbohydrates

Power breakfast with eggs, chorizo sausage and tomatoes

Ingredients for 4 people

- 2 Onions
- 200 g Cherry tomatoes
- 150 g Chorizo sausage
- 2 tbsp Sunflower oil
- 4th Eggs (size M)

- 3 stem (s) basil
- salt
- pepper

preparation

25 minutes

1 Peel and halve the onions and cut into fine strips. Wash, drain and halve tomatoes. Cut the chorizo into slices. Divide the oil in 2 pans and heat.
2 Add half onions and chorizo and fry vigorously for about 2 minutes while turning, add tomatoes and beat 2 eggs in each pan. Fry for approx. 4 minutes over medium heat.
3 Wash the basil, shake dry, pluck the leaves from the stems and roughly chop. Season the eggs with salt and pepper. Arrange the pans and sprinkle with basil.

Nutritional info

1 person approx:

310 kcal1300 kJ17 g protein25 g fat4 g of carbohydrates

Yogurt rolls from the springform pan

Ingredients for 8 people

- 1 cube (42 g) yeast
- 250 g Whole wheat flour
- 400 g dark wheat flour (type 1050)
- 1 heaped teaspoon of salt
- 75 g sugar
- 400 g Whole milk yogurt
- 3 tbsp olive oil
- 1 tbsp Poppy
- 2 tbsp Sunflower seeds

- 1-2 tbsp Sesame seeds
- Flour
- fat

preparation

45 minutes

1. Stir the yeast and 100 ml lukewarm water until smooth. Mix the flour, salt and sugar in a bowl and make a well in the middle. Put the dissolved yeast in the middle and mix with a little flour from the edge. Cover with flour and let rise for about 15 minutes.
2. Add yoghurt and olive oil to the pre-dough and knead with the dough hook of the hand mixer to form a smooth dough. Cover the dough with foil and let rise in the refrigerator overnight.
3. Knead the dough on a floured work surface and divide into 8 equal pieces. Shape dough pieces into round rolls, then brush with water. Sprinkle with poppy seeds, sunflower seeds or sesame seeds as desired. Place the rolls in a greased springform pan (26 cm Ø) and let rise in a warm place for 30–45 minutes until the rolls have enlarged significantly.
4. Bake in a preheated oven (electric stove: 200 ° C / convection: 175 ° C / gas: level 3) for about 25 minutes. Remove the rolls, let them cool for about 10 minutes and remove them from the edge. Let cool on a wire rack. Quark with cherry jam tastes good with it.

Nutritional info

1 portion approx:

400 kcal1680 kJ13 g protein10 g fat67 g of carbohydrates

Salmon and horseradish canapes

Ingredients for 6 people

- 4-5 tbsp oil
- 1/2 Baguette bread
- 250 g Double cream cream cheese
- 1 tsp Horseradish (glass)
- 1/2 tsp Dijon mustard
- Splash of lemon juice
- pepper
- salt
- 50 g fresh baby spinach

- 250 g Sliced smoked salmon
- Organic lime

preparation

25 minutes

1. Cut the baguette bread into 16 thin slices. Heat the oil in portions in a large pan. Roast the bread slices in portions for 1–2 minutes on each side
2. Mix the cream cheese with the horseradish and mustard. Season to taste with lemon juice, pepper and salt. Wash baby spinach and pat dry. Finely chop 20 g spinach and stir into the cream cheese
3. Spread the cream cheese cream on the bread slices, top with the remaining spinach flakes and smoked salmon. Wash the lime, rub dry and peel off the peel in fine strips with a zest zipper. Sprinkle the salmon with it

Nutritional info

1 person approx:

220 kcal920 kJ10 g protein16 g fat9 g of carbohydrates

Eggs benedict

Ingredients for 4 people

- 4 tbsp vinegar
- salt
- 4th Eggs (size M)
- avocado
- 2 tbsp Lemon juice
- slices (approx. 20 g each) boiled ham
- 1/4 bunch chives
- 150 g butter
- 2 Egg yolk (size M)
- 1 tbsp Cream yogurt
- 2 Wheat toasties (approx. 50 g each)
- pepper

preparation

25 minutes

1. Boil approx. 3 liters of water in a saucepan. Add vinegar and salt. Beat eggs one at a time in a cup. Use a whisk to create a strudel in the vinegar water and slide the eggs one by one into the strudel. Cook in it for about 4 minutes. Lift out and drain on kitchen paper.

2. Halve the avocado, remove the stone, remove the pulp from the skin and cut into wedges. Drizzle with 1 tablespoon of lemon juice. Halve the ham slices. Wash the chives, shake dry and cut into fine rolls.

3. Melt the butter. For the sauce, stir the egg yolks, yoghurt, 1 pinch of salt and 1 tablespoon of lemon juice in a tall, narrow mug with the hand blender. Slowly pour the butter into the egg yolk mixture. Continue pureeing until a smooth sauce is obtained.

4. Halve toasties and toast. Cover the halves of the toast with ham, avocado and eggs, sprinkle with chives and drizzle with the sauce. Sprinkle with coarse pepper.

Nutritional info

1 piece approx:

640 kcal2680 kJ18 g protein57 g fat12 g of carbohydrates

Fleet Franzbrötchen

Ingredients for 9 people

- 1 pack (530 g each) Yeast cake batter (cooling shelf)
- 50 g soft butter
- 150 g Strawberry Jam
- 1 Egg (size M)
- 1 tbsp milk
- 1-2 tbsp Granulated sugar
- Parchment paper

preparation

45 minutes

1. Preheat the oven (electric stove: 180 ° C / convection: 160 ° C / gas: see manufacturer). Line two trays with baking paper. Unroll the dough and spread the butter on top. Stir the jam until smooth and spread it on top as well. Roll up the dough from the long side.

2. Alternately cut the rolling pin diagonally into about 9 pieces so that one side of the pieces is 3 cm long and the other 5 cm long. Place on the baking sheets with the broad side down. Press in the middle. Whisk the egg and milk together and brush the Franzbrötchen with it. Sprinkle with granulated sugar. Bake in a hot oven for about 15 minutes until golden brown.

Nutritional info

1 piece approx:

240 kcal5 g protein8 g of fat36 g of carbohydrates

Scrambled eggs with stremel salmon

Ingredients for 4 people

- 8th Eggs
- 100 ml milk
- Salt pepper
- 50 g Mung bean sprouts
- 2 Spring onions
- 2 stem / s mint
- 3-4 stems coriander
- 2 tbsp oil
- 200 g Stremel salmon

preparation

15 minutes

1   Whisk eggs and milk together. Season with salt and pepper. Sort the sprouts, rinse and drain. Clean and wash the spring onions and cut into rings. Wash herbs, shake dry and pluck.

2   Heat oil in a large pan. Pour in the egg-milk mix and prepare scrambled eggs, stirring occasionally. Tear up the salmon and serve with the sprouts, spring onions and herbs. This goes well with Sriracha sauce and lime juice.

Nutritional info

1 portion approx:

360 kcal26 g protein25 g fat4 g of carbohydrates

Pancake tower with fruit salad

Ingredients for 7 people

- 5 tbsp butter or margarine
- 250 g Flour
- 1 tsp baking powder
- 100 g sugar
- packages Vanillin sugar
- 1 pinch salt
- 3 Eggs (size M)
- 400 ml milk
- 2 tbsp Clarified butter
- 250 g Whole milk couverture chips
- 2 Bananas (approx. 150 g each)

- 2 Apples (approx. 200 g each)
- 2 Oranges (approx. 200 g each)
- 2 Kiwis (approx. 125 g each)
- 5 tbsp orange juice
- 5 tbsp honey

preparation

30 minutes

1   Melt fat. Mix the flour, baking powder, sugar, vanilla sugar and salt. Whisk the eggs with a whisk. Stir in milk and liquid fat. Gradually stir in the flour mixture, tablespoon at a time. Heat a little clarified butter in a coated pan (approx. 18 cm Ø) and add 1/8 of the batter.

2   Fry the pancakes over medium heat for about 3 minutes on each side until golden brown. Place the baked pancakes on top of each other on a plate and sprinkle with chocolate chips, except for the last one. Keep warm in the preheated oven (electric stove: approx. 50 ° C).

3   Bake the rest of the dough in the same way, adding a little clarified butter in portions. Peel the bananas and cut into pieces. Wash the apples, pat dry, quarter them, remove the core and cut the pulp into pieces. Peel the oranges and kiwis and cut the pulp into pieces.

4   Mix the prepared fruit with orange juice and honey in a bowl. If you like, add more honey to taste.

Divide the pancake tower into 6-8 servings. Serve with fruit salad

Nutritional info

1 person approx:

560 kcal2350 kJ10 g protein23 g fat76 g of carbohydrates

Apple and cinnamon popovers

Ingredients for 12 people

- 1 Apple (e.g. Braeburn)
- 1 tsp cinnamon
- 2 tsp sugar
- 25 g Raisins
- 15 g butter or margarine
- 3 tsp oil
- eggs at room temperature (size M)
- 250 ml room temperature milk
- salt
- 125 g Flour

preparation

45 minutes

1 Wash the apple, rub dry and cut into quarters. Remove the core casing. Cut 2 quarters into cubes, use the remaining quarters for other purposes. Mix the cinnamon and sugar. Mix the apple cubes with the raisins and 2/3 of the cinnamon-sugar mixture. Melt the fat in a small saucepan and let cool down a little. Put 1/2 teaspoon of oil in each of the 12 hollows of a popover tray. Place the tray in the preheated oven (electric stove: 225 ° C / convection: 200 ° C / gas: see manufacturer)

2 Briefly beat the eggs, milk, fat and 1/2 teaspoon salt with the whisk. Add the flour all at once and stir until the dough just doesn't have any lumps. Don't stir too long! Pour the batter into a measuring cup

3 Take the tray out of the oven. Fill 1/3 of each well with batter. Sprinkle the apple and raisin mixture on top and pour the remaining batter over it. Bake immediately in the hot oven for about 15 minutes. Then reduce the temperature (electric stove: 175 ° C / convection: 150 ° C / gas: see manufacturer) and bake for another 10–12 minutes. Do not open the oven door during the entire baking time. Serve the popovers warm and sprinkle with the remaining cinnamon sugar

Nutritional info

1 piece approx:

110 kcal460 kJ3 g protein6 g fat11 g of carbohydrates

Berry smoothie with granola

Ingredients for 4 people

- 3 Bananas
- 100 g Almond kernels
- 100 g Pumpkin seeds
- 125 g hearty oat flakes
- 3 tbsp oil
- 1 packet Vanillin sugar
- salt
- 5 tbsp Liquid honey
- 250 g Raspberries
- 300 g frozen blueberries
- 80 ml Almond drink
- 50 g Coconut chips

- 2 tbsp Chia seeds
- Parchment paper

preparation

45 minutes

1. The day before, peel and slice 2 bananas. Put in a bowl and freeze overnight.
2. Roughly chop the almonds for the granola. Mix with pumpkin seeds and oatmeal in a bowl. Put the oil, vanilla sugar, a pinch of salt and 2 tablespoons of honey in a small saucepan. Heat over medium heat and stir until the vanillin sugar is dissolved (do not bring to the boil). Pour over the hearty mixture and mix everything thoroughly with a wooden spoon until the dry ingredients are completely coated.
3. Place on a baking sheet lined with baking paper and distribute well. Bake in a preheated oven (electric stove: 150 ° C / convection: 125 ° C / gas: see manufacturer) for about 20 minutes until golden yellow. Turn with a wooden spoon after approx. 10 minutes. Take the baking sheet out of the oven and let the granola cool down.
4. Sort the raspberries. Put the frozen bananas, 200 g raspberries, frozen blueberries, almond drink and 3 tablespoons honey in a blender and mix until a creamy consistency is obtained. Fill the berry smoothie into bowls. Peel and slice 1 banana. Spread the banana slices, remaining raspberries,

coconut chips and granola on the smoothie and sprinkle with chia seeds.

Nutritional info

1 person approx:

460 kcal1930 kJ13 g protein24 g fat47 g of carbohydrates

Sweet potato waffles with avocado and egg

Ingredients for 4 people

- 500 g Sweet potatoes
- 6th Eggs
- 100 g Parmesan or vegetarian hard cheese
- 4 tbsp Flour
- 1 pinch (s) Paprika powder
- 1 pinch (s) grated nutmeg
- salt
- pepper
- 2 Avocados
- 5 tbsp Olive oil for the waffle iron
- Waffle maker
- cress

preparation

60 minutes

1   For the waffle batter, wash the sweet potatoes, cut in half and place on a baking sheet. Sprinkle the sweet potato halves with a pinch of salt and bake in the preheated oven (electric stove: 200 ° C / convection: 175 ° C / gas: see manufacturer) for 30-40 minutes until the sweet potato pulp is soft. Then let it cool down briefly, scrape the meat of the sweet potatoes out of the skin and mash them in a bowl.

2   Grate the parmesan and add to the sweet potatoes. Add two eggs, flour, a pinch of nutmeg and paprika powder and mix into a homogeneous batter and season with salt and pepper.

3   Heat a waffle iron, brush with olive oil and put two tablespoons of batter on it. Close the waffle iron and wait until the waffles are crispy.

4   In the meantime, heat 3 tablespoons of olive oil in a pan, slide in the remaining eggs and fry over medium heat for about 2 minutes. Season with salt and pepper.

5   Remove the avocados from the core, peel, cut into slices and arrange on 4 separate plates with the waffles and fried eggs. Garnish with cress as desired.

Nutritional info

1 portion approx:

630 kcal25 g protein35 g fat49 g of carbohydrates

Cragel: croissant and bagel

Ingredients for 4 people

- 1 Egg (size M)
- 1/2 tsp sugar
- 1 pinch salt
- 1 can (250 g) Chilled fresh dough for 6 croissants
- 1 tsp Peeled sesame seeds
- Parchment paper

preparation

30 minutes

1   Whisk the egg, sugar, salt and 1 tbsp water together.
    Open the can, unroll the dough and cut across into
    4 equal-sized rectangles (ignore perforations). Fold

over the rectangles by a third on both long sides. Pull the strips to a length of 14–15 cm and twist them in like a cord. Fold into a ring and important: press the ends together well.

2   Boil plenty of water in a large saucepan. Place the dough rings in with a slotted spoon and let them steep for about 30 seconds on each side over medium heat. Immediately lift out with a skimmer and place on a baking sheet lined with baking paper.

3   Brush cragel with the egg mixture and sprinkle with sesame seeds. Bake in the preheated oven, 2nd rail from the bottom (electric stove: 200 ° C / convection: 175 ° C / gas: see manufacturer) for about 20 minutes.

Nutritional info

1 piece approx:

240 kcal1000 kJ7 g protein13 g fat25 g of carbohydrates

Breakfast muffin burger

Ingredients for 4 people

- 150 g soft butter
- 85 g Ricotta cheese
- salt
- 11 Eggs (size M)
- 150 g Flour
- 1/2 packet baking powder
- 125 g cheddar cheese
- 35 g Parmesan cheese
- 1 clove of garlic
- 40 g sun-dried tomatoes in oil

- 200 g Sour cream
- 2 tbsp Liquid honey
- 2 tbsp Tomato paste
- pepper
- 150 g Mushrooms
- 50 g Baby leaf salad mix
- 8th Cherry tomatoes
- 4 tbsp oil
- avocado
- 1 splash Lemon juice
- 8th Paper baking cases
- Wooden skewers

preparation

75 minutes

1   Mix the butter, ricotta and a pinch of salt with the whisk of the hand mixer until creamy. Mix in 3 eggs one after the other. Mix flour and baking powder, add and stir in briefly. Grate both types of cheese and fold into the batter.

2   Line 8 wells of a muffin tray (12 wells of approx. 100 ml each) with 1 paper baking dish each. Spread the dough in the wells and bake in the preheated oven (electric stove: 175 ° C / convection: 150 ° C / gas: see manufacturer) for about 20 minutes.

3   Peel garlic and chop finely. Drain the dried tomatoes in a colander and finely dice. Mix the sour cream, honey, tomato paste, tomatoes and garlic, season

with salt and pepper. Clean, clean and slice the mushrooms. Wash the lettuce and pat dry. Take the muffins out of the oven and let them cool down a little. Take the muffins out of the wells and let them cool on a wire rack.

4   Wash tomatoes. Heat 2 tablespoons of oil in a pan, fry the mushrooms and tomatoes vigorously for about 2 minutes while turning, season with salt and pepper. Heat 2 tablespoons of oil in another pan and fry the eggs in portions with the help of round fried egg molds, season with pepper.

5   Halve the avocado along the core, remove the core and skin, cut the pulp into thin slices and drizzle with lemon juice. Cut the muffins horizontally and brush with the sour cream. Layer the lettuce, mushrooms, avocado and fried egg on top, put the lid on top. Place the tomatoes on the lid and secure with 1 wooden skewer each.

Nutritional info

1 piece approx:

630 kcal2640 kJ21 g protein51 g fat20 g of carbohydrates

Pancake hearts with maple syrup and apricot compote

Ingredients for 4 people

- 1 can (s) (425 ml) apricots
- 1 packet "Vanilla flavor" sauce powder
- 200 ml orange juice
- 3 Eggs (size M)
- 100 ml milk
- 150 g Whole milk yogurt
- 150 g Flour

- 1 packet baking powder
- 1 pinch salt
- 2 tbsp sugar
- 2 tbsp oil
- 6 stem (s) Lemon balm
- 1 tbsp powdered sugar
- 100 ml Maple syrup
- 1 tbsp ground pistachio nuts

preparation

60 minutes

1   For the compote, drain the apricots while collecting the juice. Mix the sauce powder and 100 ml orange juice until smooth. Bring 100 ml orange juice and the collected apricot juice to the boil, remove from the heat. Stir in the mixed sauce powder, bring to the boil briefly while stirring, remove from the stove. Halve the apricot halves, mix with the orange sauce, leave to cool

2   Beat eggs with the whisk of the hand mixer to a light, frothy cream. Mix milk and yoghurt, mix flour and baking powder. Gradually add the flour and milk mixture, salt and sugar to the custard and stir to a thick batter

3   Oil the inside of 3 metal heart cutters. Heat a little oil in a non-stick pan over medium heat. Place the molds in the pan, pour in the dough in portions. Let the dough set for 2-3 minutes, carefully loosen the

molds with a knife if necessary. Turn the pancakes over and bake on the other side until golden brown. Keep the pancakes warm and process the remaining batter in the same way so that a total of 12 pancakes are baked

4   Wash lemon balm, pat dry, set something aside for garnish. Cut the rest into fine strips and add to the compote. Dust the pancakes with powdered sugar. Drizzle with maple syrup and serve with compote. Sprinkle with pistachios and decorate with lemon balm

Nutritional info

1 person approx:

530 kcal2220 kJ13 g protein14 g fat

Grapefruit and banana jam

Ingredients for 5 people

- 4th Pink grapefruits
- 3 yellow grapefruit
- 1 pack Preserving sugar 2: 1
- 2 Bananas
- 1/2 tsp cinnamon

preparation

30 minutes

1   Peel the grapefruit with a knife so that the white skin is also removed. Cut out the fillets. Squeeze the juice out of the dividing walls and the remains of the peel and collect it. Weigh out approx. 750 g of pulp and juice, mix with the preserving sugar in a large saucepan.

2   Peel the bananas, weigh 250 g and cut into slices. Heat the grapefruit and sugar mixture while stirring. Cook over high heat while stirring for about 2 minutes. Add the bananas and cinnamon, cook for a further 1–2 minutes (gel test!).

3   Pour hot into clean, dry glasses. Immediately close the jars tightly, turn them upside down for about 10 minutes, then turn them over and let them cool.

Cloud eggs

Ingredients for 4 people

- Parchment paper
- 4th Eggs (size M)
- 1 tbsp grated parmesan or vegetarian hard cheese
- pepper

preparation

15 minutes

1   Preheat the oven for 4 people (electric stove: 200 °
    C / convection: 180 ° C / gas: see manufacturer). Line
    a baking sheet with parchment paper. Separate 4
    eggs (size M), put the egg yolks aside in the shell

halves (e.g., in the egg box). Beat the egg whites until stiff.

2   Fold in 1 tablespoon of grated parmesan. Spread the egg whites in 4 piles on the tray. Press a teaspoon into the center. Bake in the hot oven for about 6 minutes. Let the egg yolks slide into the hollows and bake for another 3 minutes. Season with pepper.

3   Also tastes good sprinkled with herbs on toasted bread with crispy bacon.

Nutritional info

1 portion approx:

95 kcal8 g protein6 g fat1 g of carbohydrates

Heavenly millet porridge

Ingredients for 2 people

- 100 g Millet flakes
- 100 g Frozen raspberries
- 100 g Greek cream yogurt
- 2-3 tbsp Frozen blueberries
- 1 tbsp Cocoa nibs (cocoa nibs)
- cinnamon
- 1-2 tbsp Agave syrup

preparation

15 minutes

1   Bring 1/2 l of water to the boil. Stir in millet flakes
    and simmer for 1–2 minutes while stirring. Add the

frozen raspberries and continue stirring over low heat until the porridge turns pink.

2　Fill porridge into bowls. Serve with the yogurt and the frozen blueberries. Chop the cocoa nibs and sprinkle with a little cinnamon. Drizzle with agave syrup if you like. Serve immediately.

Nutritional info

1 portion approx:

200 kcal5 g protein6 g fat28 g of carbohydrates

Raisin bread with cream cheese

Ingredients for 6 people

- 4th Eggs (size M)
- 100 ml + 2 tbsp milk
- 1 packet Vanillin sugar
- 6 slices Raisin bread (approx. 60 g each)
- 200 g Double cream cheese
- 125 g Lemon curd
- 1 1/2 tsp cinnamon
- 2-3 tbsp sugar
- 25 g Clarified butter

preparation

20 minutes

1 For the egg milk, whisk the eggs, 100 ml milk and vanilla sugar. Place the bread slices side by side in a flat dish. Pour the egg milk evenly over it and let it steep for about 15 minutes. Turn the bread slices halfway through

2 In the meantime, mix the cream cheese, lemon curd and 2 tablespoons of milk. Mix the cinnamon and sugar. Heat the clarified butter in two portions in a large pan, fry 3 slices of bread one after the other while turning until golden yellow and remove.

3 Halve as desired, arrange on a platter sprinkled with a dollop of cream cheese and cinnamon sugar. Taste warm and cold

Nutritional info

1 person approx:

410 kcal1720 kJ12 g protein15 g fat55 g of carbohydrates

Baked grapefruit with oatmeal crunch

Ingredients for 4 people

- 40 g hearty oat flakes
- 4 tbsp + about 8 tsp maple syrup
- 5g butter
- 1 pink grapefruit
- 1 yellow grapefruit
- 4 tbsp Brown sugar
- 150 g Cream yogurt
- oil
- Aluminum foil

preparation

25 minutes

1   Coat a piece of aluminum foil thinly with oil. Caramelize the oatmeal and 3 tbsp maple syrup in a non-stick pan. Finally add the butter, stir in briefly and distribute the oatmeal crunch on the aluminum foil. Let cool down.

2   Halve the grapefruit crosswise. If desired, remove the individual segments from the separating membranes and the shell with a sharp knife.

3   Line a baking sheet with aluminum foil, place the grapefruit halves on top and sprinkle each half with 1 teaspoon of brown sugar and drizzle with 1 teaspoon of maple syrup. Gratinate for approx. 10 minutes under the preheated grill.

4   Serve the finished grapefruit halves with 1 tbsp cream yoghurt and oatmeal crunch. Drizzle with 1 teaspoon of maple syrup each.

Nutritional info

1 person approx:

280 kcal1170 kJ4 g protein6 g fat51 g of carbohydrates

Cheddar Farls with fried egg and crispy bacon

Ingredients for 4 people

- 450 g Wheat flour plus flour for processing
- 1 packet baking powder
- 1 tsp Baking soda, 1 teaspoon salt
- 1 tsp English mustard powder (alternatively finely ground mustard seeds)
- 2 tsp yellow mustard seeds, roughly ground
- 150 g Cheese, grated (e.g. cheddar)
- 280 ml Buttermilk
- 90 ml Whole milk
- 4th Panicles of cherry tomatoes
- olive oil

- Salt, black pepper
- 12th thick slices of bacon
- 4th Eggs (size L)
- Sunflower oil
- butter

preparation

40 minutes

1. Preheat the oven to 220 ° C (fan oven 200 ° C). Sift the flour, baking powder, baking soda, salt and mustard powder into a bowl. Mix in the mustard seeds and cheese. Pour in the buttermilk and milk and work everything into a soft, sticky dough.
2. Work the dough quickly on the floured worktop (Ø 22 cm), place on a lightly floured baking sheet and cut into 8 pieces of cake. Pull the pieces apart, dust them lightly with flour and bake until golden brown in 20 minutes.
3. In the meantime, place the cherry tomatoes in a small ovenproof dish, drizzle with olive oil and season with salt and pepper. After 10 minutes of baking time, add to the Farls in the oven and bake for 10 minutes.
4. In the meantime, heat a (grill) pan at a high temperature until it smokes. Reduce to medium heat and fry the bacon in it until crispy. At the same time, fry the fried eggs in a second pan in sunflower oil as desired.

5   (We like crispy edges and egg yolks that are still runny.) Season with salt and pepper.

6   Take the finished farls out of the oven, cut a pocket into each piece from the tip, brush with butter and fill with bacon and eggs. Serve with the tomatoes.

Nutritional info

1 piece approx:

310 kcal13 g protein15 g fat29 g of carbohydrates

Filled almond croissants

Ingredients for 6 people

- 60 g soft butter
- 50 g sugar
- 1 Egg (size M)
- a few drops Bitter almond flavor
- 80 g ground almonds
- 1 tsp Flour
- 6th croissants
- 20 g Almond flakes
- 2 tbsp powdered sugar
- Parchment paper

preparation

20 minutes

1 Mix the soft butter and sugar until creamy. Stir in egg and bitter almond flavor one after the other. Mix and stir in the ground almonds and flour.

2 Preheat the oven (electric stove: 180 ° C / convection: 160 ° C / gas: see manufacturer). Line a tray with baking paper. Cut the croissants lengthways. Fill with some almond cream and distribute the rest on the croissants. Sprinkle with flaked almonds and bake in the oven for 10–15 minutes. Dust with powdered sugar.

3 You can use croissants from the day before.

Nutritional info

1 piece approx:

1 kcal1 g protein1 g fat1 g of carbohydrates

Breakfast bowl with banana and granola

Ingredients for 4 people

- 150 g Oat flakes (coarse and fine mixed)
- 25 g Pumpkin seeds
- 50 g Desiccated coconut
- 50 g sliced almonds
- 20 g Amaranth
- 20 g shaved hazelnuts
- 30 g Coconut oil
- 5 tbsp honey
- 1 pinch (s) cinnamon
- 1 pck. Vanillin sugar
- 500 g Greek yogurt (10% fat)

- 4th Bananas
- 50 g Blueberries
- Kiwi fruit
- 1 tbsp Maple syrup
- mint
- Parchment paper

preparation

45 minutes

1   For the granola, put oat flakes, pumpkin seeds, grated almonds and hazelnuts, desiccated coconut, amaranth, cinnamon, vanilla sugar in a bowl and mix with honey and coconut oil.

2   Place the granola on a baking sheet with baking paper and bake in a preheated oven (electric stove: 200 ° C / convection: 175 ° C / gas: see manufacturer) for 20-30 minutes. Take out and let cool down.

3   In the meantime, wash the blueberries and peel the kiwis and bananas. Cut the kiwi fruit into fine cubes, divide the bananas lengthways.

4   Spread 4 tablespoons of Greek yogurt in each of 4 cereal bowls. Place the kiwi cubes, blueberries and 2 banana slices on top. Sprinkle with 3 tablespoons of granola, drizzle 1 tablespoon of maple syrup and garnish with fresh mint.

Nutritional info

1 portion approx:

810 kcal21 g protein43 g fat78 g of carbohydrates

Breakfast burrito with bacon and avocado salad

Ingredients for 4 people

- 4 slices Breakfast bacon
- 2 tbsp freshly squeezed lemon juice
- salt
- Chili powder
- 1 tbsp honey
- 3 tbsp olive oil
- 1 small shallot
- 100 g Rocket
- (each 14 cm Ø) Tortillas

- 1 ripe avocado
- Parchment paper
- Tapes

preparation

30 minutes

1. Fry the bacon in a pan without fat until crispy while turning. Remove and drain on kitchen paper. For the vinaigrette, whisk together lemon juice, salt, chilli and honey. Beat in the oil drop by drop.
2. Peel the shallot, cut into fine cubes and stir into the vinaigrette. Clean rocket, wash and spin dry. Toast the tortillas in the pan in portions for 1 minute on each side.
3. Halve the avocado, remove the stone, remove the pulp from the skin and cut into wedges. Top the tortillas with rocket, bacon and lettuce and drizzle with vinaigrette. Roll up tortillas into burritos, wrap with parchment paper and tie with ribbons.

Nutritional info

1 person approx:

370 kcal1550 kJ8 g protein26 g fat28 g of carbohydrates

Oatmeal crumble with rhubarb

Ingredients for 4 people

- 3 sticks (250 g each) rhubarb
- 100 g blueberries
- 2 Bananas
- 300 g hearty oat flakes
- 1 tbsp Coconut oil
- 3 tbsp Liquid honey
- 5 tbsp Brown sugar
- 500 ml Almond drink

preparation

60 minutes

1 Clean, peel and cut the rhubarb into large pieces. Sort the blueberries, wash and drain well. Peel the bananas and cut into slices at an angle. Mix together the oat flakes, coconut oil, honey, 4 tbsp sugar, fruits and rhubarb.
2 Pour the mixture into a baking dish (approx. 1 1/2 l) and pour the almond drink over it. Sprinkle with 1 tablespoon of sugar. Bake in a preheated oven (electric stove: 175 ° C / convection: 150 ° C / gas: see manufacturer) for about 40 minutes. Take the crumble out of the oven and serve.

Nutritional info

1 portion approx:

520 kcal11 g protein11 g fat90 g of carbohydrates

Straw widower bread with fried egg

Ingredients for 1 person

- 1 glass (125 g) "Pure early carrots" (e.g. from Hipp)
- Salt pepper
- 1 tsp Sambal Oelek
- 3 tbsp butter
- 1 slice farmers bread
- 2 Eggs
- 3-4 Chives stalks

preparation

1 Season the carrots with salt and sambal oelek. Heat 1 tbsp butter in a pan. Roast bread in it for about 2

minutes on each side until golden brown and remove. Heat 1 tbsp butter in the frying fat. Beat in eggs one by one.

2   Fry them with fried eggs. Season with salt and pepper.

3   Wash the chives, shake dry and cut into fine rolls. Spread the carrot mix on the bread and arrange the fried eggs on top. Sprinkle with chives.

Nutritional info

1 person approx:

580 kcal21 g protein35 g fat41 g of carbohydrates

Scrambled eggs with toasted wholemeal bread strips

Ingredients for 2 people

- 2 discs Whole grain bread
- 1/4 bunch chives
- 200 g Cherry tomatoes
- 1 tsp olive oil
- 2 Eggs (size M)
- 100 ml Skimmed milk (0.3% fat)
- salt

- pepper

preparation

15 minutes

Cut bread into cubes. Toast in a pan without fat over medium heat for about 5 minutes until crispy. Wash the chives, shake dry, save for something to garnish, cut into rolls.

Wash tomatoes and cut in half. Take the bread out of the pan. Heat oil, add tomatoes and stew for 1 minute. Put the bread back in the pan. Whisk eggs, chives and milk together. Season with salt and pepper.

Pour the egg into the pan and let it set while stirring. Cut the remaining chives a little smaller. Arrange the scrambled eggs on plates and garnish with chives.

Nutritional info

1 person approx:

230 kcal960 kJ13 g protein10 g fat21 g of carbohydrates

Spinach and goat cheese rolls

Ingredients for 12 people

- 400 g young spinach
- salt
- 450 g Flour
- 1 packet Dry yeast
- 1 tsp sugar
- 150 g Whole milk yogurt
- 4 tbsp Corn grits
- 3 tbsp Sunflower oil
- 300 g tomatoes

- 1 small red onion
- pepper
- 2 tbsp Wine vinegar
- 150 g Goat cream cheese

preparation

50 minutes

1. Sort the spinach, wash it and, except for 24 beautiful leaves, blanch it in boiling salted water for about 1 minute. Pour the spinach into a sieve, rinse in cold water and drain well. Chop the spinach very finely

2. Knead the flour, yeast, 1/2 teaspoon salt, sugar, spinach and yoghurt with the dough hook of the hand mixer to form a smooth dough. Depending on the consistency, add 4–6 tablespoons of water. Shape the dough into a ball and let rise in a warm place for about 1 hour

3. Knead the dough and roll out about 2 cm thick on the worktop sprinkled with semolina. Use a round cutter (approx. 8 cm Ø) to cut out approx. 12 rolls, kneading the leftovers over and over again. Cover with a cloth and let rise for another 30 minutes

4. Heat 1 tablespoon of oil in each of 2 large pans and fry / bake the rolls over medium heat for about 12 minutes, turning. In the meantime, wash, clean and dice tomatoes. Peel the onion and cut into cubes. Season the tomatoes and onions with salt, pepper, vinegar and 1 tablespoon of oil

5   Cut the finished rolls horizontally as required, brush with cheese and bake in a preheated oven (electric stove: 225 ° C / convection: 200 ° C / gas: see manufacturer) for about 4 minutes. Serve with spinach and tomato salad

Nutritional info

1 piece approx:

200 kcal840 kJ6 g protein5 g of fat32 g of carbohydrates

Morning greenie

Ingredients for 4 people

- 50 g Broccoli florets
- 30 g Baby spinach
- 3 stem (s) Lemon balm
- 1/2 kiwi
- 1/2 avocado
- 1/2 tbsp ground almonds
- 1 tbsp Lemons
- 150 ml Apple juice

preparation

10 mins

1. Wash broccoli florets and cook in salted boiling water for 6–8 minutes until soft. Drain, rinse in cold water and let cool down. Sort out baby spinach, wash and drain.
2. Wash lemon balm, shake dry and pick off the leaves. Peel 1/2 kiwi, cut into small pieces. Remove 1/2 avocado from the skin, cut into small pieces. Put all ingredients in a tall mixing bowl with 1/2 tbsp ground almonds, 1 tbsp lemon and 150 ml apple juice.
3. Puree finely with a hand blender or in a stand mixer. Pour into a glass and serve immediately.

Nutritional info

1 portion approx:

310 kcal6 g protein22 g fat20 g of carbohydrates

Fried egg toast with bacon and maple syrup

Ingredients for 4 people

- 1⁄2 bunch chives
- 4 slices Whole grain toast
- 8 slices Bacon
- 2 tsp butter
- 4th Eggs
- pepper
- 1 tbsp Maple syrup to drizzle

preparation

20 minutes

1 Wash the chives, shake dry and cut into fine rolls. Cut out a circle (approx. 5 cm Ø) in the middle of each slice of toast.
2 Fry the bacon in a large non-stick pan until crispy. Take out, keep warm. Heat 1 teaspoon butter in the bacon fat. Add 2 bread circles and 2 bread slices each. Beat 2 eggs and place on the bread slices.
3 Fry for 1–2 minutes over low to medium heat. Turn and fry again for 1–2 minutes. Season with pepper. Keep warm or fry all the breads and bread circles in two pans at the same time.
4 Arrange the bread with bread circles and bacon. Possibly drizzle maple syrup over it and sprinkle with chives.

Nutritional info

1 piece approx:

270 kcal 13 g protein 17 g fat 15 g of carbohydrates

Bircher muesli with papaya and honey

Ingredients for 1 person

- 5g Sunflower seeds
- 25 g delicate oat flakes
- 2 tbsp low-fat milk (1.5% fat)
- 50 g Skimmed milk yogurt (0.3% fat)
- 1/2 (approx. 200 g) papaya
- 10 g Liquid honey

preparation

10 mins

1   Roast the sunflower seeds in a pan without fat, remove them immediately and let them cool. Mix together the oatmeal, milk and yoghurt and place in a small bowl
2   Peel the papaya, remove the seeds and cut the pulp into cubes. Place the papaya on top of the oatmeal yogurt mixture and drizzle with honey. Sprinkle with sunflower seeds

Nutritional info

1 person approx:

190 kcal790 kJ8 g protein5 g of fat29 g of carbohydrates

Salad sandwich with 1 glass of almond drink

Ingredients for 4 people

- 125 g Cucumber
- 8th radish
- 75 g Lamb's lettuce
- 3-4 tbsp low-fat yoghurt
- Juice of 1/2 lemon
- salt
- pepper

- 8th Whole grain sandwich slices
- 4 tbsp Tomato paste
- pepper from the grinder
- 150 ml Almond drink (soy drink)

preparation

15 minutes

1   Clean and wash the cucumber and cut into thin slices. Clean, wash and slice the radishes. Thoroughly clean and wash the lamb's lettuce and drain in a sieve. For the dressing, stir together the yogurt and lemon juice until smooth, season with salt and pepper

2   Toast sandwich slices one after the other in the toaster. Brush the toast slices with 1/2 tbsp tomato paste each. Cover 4 slices of toast with lamb's lettuce, cucumber and radishes.

3   Spread the yogurt dressing on top. Cover with the remaining slices of toast. Slice the sandwich diagonally, arrange on plates and sprinkle with black pepper from the mill if you like. A glass of almond drink goes well with this

Nutritional info

1 person approx:

240 kcal1000 kJ9 g protein4 g of fat41 g of carbohydrates

Wheat rolls

Ingredients for 12 people

- 500 g Flour
- 1 1/2–2 tsp salt
- 10 g fresh yeast
- Flour
- Parchment paper

preparation

45 minutes

1   Mix the flour and salt in a bowl. Crumble the yeast and mix with 300 ml of ice-cold water. Add to the flour and knead into a smooth dough with the dough hook of the hand mixer
2   Cover and let rise in the refrigerator overnight. The next day, divide the dough into 12 equal pieces. Shape each one into a bun with floured hands. Place on two baking sheets lined with baking paper and score crosswise or lengthways as desired
3   Fill a small, ovenproof dish with water and place it in the preheated oven (electric stove: 225 ° C / fan: 200 ° C / gas: level 4). Bake the rolls in it for 12–15 minutes. Take out of the oven, place on a wire rack and cool or cool as you like. Arrange in a basket. Butter and jam go well with this

Nutritional info

1 piece approx:

140 kcal580 kJ4 g protein30 g of carbohydrates

Cheese and apple bread

Ingredients for 1 person

- 30 g Camembert (30% fat in dry matter)
- 1 tbsp (30 g) Quark (20% fat)
- salt
- 1 tbsp (10 g) Walnut kernels
- 1 (approx. 100 g) little apple
- 1 slice (50 g) Whole grain bread
- pink berries
- sage

preparation

10 mins

1. Chop the cheese into small cubes, mix with the quark and season with salt. Roughly chop the nuts. Wash and quarter the apple and remove the core. Cut the apple into wedges. Spread the cheese cream on bread, place on a plate.
2. Spread the apple wedges on the bread and plate. Sprinkle with nuts. Sprinkle with pink berries and garnish with sage.

Nutritional info

1 person approx:

310 kcal1300 kJ16 g protein13 g fat32 g of carbohydrates

Portuguese croissant with serrano and manchego

Ingredients for 6 people

- 75 ml milk
- 375 g Flour
- 1/2 cube (21 g) fresh yeast
- 75 g sugar
- 75 g butter or margarine
- 1 pinch salt
- 4th Egg yolk (size M)
- 6 slices Manchego cheese
- 12 slices Serrano ham
- Flour

- Parchment paper

preparation

40 minutes

1. Warm milk. Put the flour in a bowl, make a well in the middle and crumble the yeast into it. Add 25 g sugar and lukewarm milk and mix with a little flour from the edge to a thick paste.
2. Cover and let rise for 15-20 minutes. Add the soft fat in pieces, 50 g sugar, salt and 3 egg yolks to the pre-dough in the bowl and knead with the dough hook of the hand mixer to form a smooth yeast dough.
3. Cover and let rise for another 40 minutes. Roll out the yeast dough on a floured work surface into a rectangle (40 x 25 cm). Cut into 6 pieces of cake with a pastry knife. Roll up the pieces of dough tightly and place them on a baking sheet lined with baking paper. Let rise in a warm place for another 30 minutes.
4. Whisk 1 egg yolk and 2 tablespoons of water. Brush the croissants thinly. In the preheated oven (electric stove: 200 ° C / fan oven: 175 ° C / gas: level 3) Bake for approx. 15 minutes. Let cool down. Halve horizontally and top with cheese and ham

Nutritional info

1 piece approx:

590 kcal2470 kJ24 g protein29 g fat58 g of carbohydrates

Bread with trout cream, frisee, eggs and parsley oil

Ingredients for 2 people

2 Eggs (size M)

75 g smoked trout fillet

2 tsp Cream horseradish

3 tsp Creme fraiche Cheese

  salt

6 stem (s) parsley

3 tsp olive oil

some leaves Frisée salad

4 slices Brown bread

  black pepper

preparation

10 mins

Boil eggs in boiling water for about 6 minutes and rinse with cold water. Peel and halve the eggs. Mash the trout fillet with a fork, mix with the cream horseradish and crème fraîche. Season to taste with salt. Wash the parsley, shake dry and chop very finely, stir with olive oil and season with salt. Wash the Frisée salad, shake it dry and pluck it into small pieces

Brush bread slices with trout cream, cover with lettuce and 1/2 egg each. Drizzle with parsley oil and sprinkle with pepper

Nutritional info

1 person approx:

450 kcal1890 kJ22 g protein23 g fat35 g of carbohydrates

Roasted red pepper and tuna omelets

Ingredients for 4 people

- 2 can (s) (185 g each) tuna (in its own juice)
- 1 glass (370 ml) red roasted peppers in brine
- 2 Garlic cloves
- 40 g Parmesan cheese
- 4 tbsp oil
- 8th fresh eggs (size M)
- salt
- pepper
- 5 tbsp olive oil
- 1 Stalk thyme

preparation

25 minutes

1. Drain and tear the tuna. Drain the peppers and cut into thin strips. Peel and chop the garlic. Finely slice the parmesan
2. Heat 1 tablespoon of oil in a pan, fry the paprika in it. Add the garlic, fry for about 1 minute, place in a bowl, add the tuna and half of the parmesan. Separate eggs. Beat egg whites until stiff. Season with salt and pepper. Fold into the pepper and tuna mixture
3. Heat 1 tablespoon of oil in a pan (14.5 cm Ø) and let 1/4 of the omelette mixture set in it for 5–6 minutes. Place the omelette on a plate while still warm. Put 2 egg yolks on top. Keep warm in the oven. Process the remaining omelette mixture and eggs in the same way. Wash the thyme, pluck the leaves and sprinkle over the omelets. Scatter the remaining parmesan shavings on top and serve

Nutritional info

1 person approx:

470 kcal1970 kJ36 g protein33 g fat6 g of carbohydrates

Avocado and pea cream

Ingredients for 6 people

- 200 g frozen peas
- salt
- 2 ripe avocados (approx. 250 g each; e.g. Ryan)
- 1 federal government coriander
- Juice of 1 lime
- pepper

preparation

15 minutes

1   Cook the peas in boiling salted water for about 5 minutes. Drain and chill cold. Halve the avocados, remove the seeds. Remove the pulp from the skin and mash or mash with the peas in a bowl. Wash the coriander, pat dry.
2   Pluck leaves and finely chop. Mix with the avovado cream with the lime juice, season with salt and pepper. Bread tastes good with it

Nutritional info

1 person approx:

160 kcal670 kJ3 g protein15 g fat5 g of carbohydrates

Crispbread with almond cream cheese

Ingredients for 1 person

- 1 tbsp Almond kernels with skin
- 1 tsp Pistachio nuts
- 100 g Cream cheese (21% fat)
- 1 slice (14 g) Sesame crispbread
- 1 Lettuce leaf
- (5 g each) Sesame crisps
- 1 tsp honey

- 200 ml Skimmed milk (0.3% fat)
- 75 g Raspberries
- Lemon balm

preparation

12 minutes

1. Chop the almonds and pistachios and mix with the cream cheese. Cover the slice of crispbread with lettuce leaves. Spread the cream cheese on all crispbreads.
2. Drizzle with honey. Puree the milk and raspberries in a blender. Serve the drink and crispbread garnished with lemon balm

Nutritional info

1 person approx:

450 kcal1890 kJ26 g protein20 g fat41 g of carbohydrates

CONCLUSION

The food eaten at this time has a decisive influence on the body's physiological response, both physically and mentally. Breakfast is considered one of the most important intakes of the day for several reasons, one of them because it provides the energy and nutrients that the body needs to start the day and helps to reorganize the metabolic changes that have occurred during the night.

While we sleep, the energy reserves provided at dinner have been used up and it is necessary to renew them before starting any activity. We need carbohydrates, which are transformed into glucose, which is our fuel and allows our brain to function properly. We also need fiber for intestinal function, that is, to avoid problems such as constipation. Or vitamins, keys to multiple functions, such as intellectual performance and mood; and minerals, necessary for the growth and maintenance of bones and teeth, but also for the muscles.